Inspiring Anecdotes

from the lives of great men

J.M. Mehta

Publisher
UNICORN BOOKS

F-2/16, Ansari Road, Daryaganj, New Delhi-110002
☎ 011-23275434, 23262683, 23250704 • *Fax:* 011-23257790
E-mail: info@unicornbooks.in • *Website:* www.unicornbooks.in

Branch : Mumbai
23-25, Zaoba Wadi, Thakurdwar, Mumbai-401002
☎ 022-22010941, 022-22053387
E-mail: rapidex@bom5.vsnl.net.in

ISBN 978-81-7806-133-7

Edition : 2015

Printed at : Param Offsetters, Okhla, New Delhi-110020

Preface

Millions of people are born in this world and then they vanish, after a short or long sojourn. Most of them are soon forgotten and are never remembered thereafter. However, there are a few exceptions – thinkers, philosophers, leaders, holy men, scientists and others who fall in a similar category. All such great people leave their footprints on the sands of time. Their names are recorded in the annals of history in golden letters. Their thoughts, teachings and certain incidents occurring in their lifetime are long remembered, even centuries after they have disappeared from the worldly scene.

Such inspiring anecdotes from the lives of great people serve as a beacon light for generations that follow. They contain instant lessons of life which are generally not found in school or college textbooks.

This book contains around a 100 such thought-provoking anecdotes gleaned from the lives of various great men of the world. The book is, therefore, meant to be read again and again, as it is full of life-related inspirational knowledge and wisdom. There is no hesitation in my mind in saying that it will guide and help the general reader in his worldly struggle and will inspire him to achieve greater progress and success in all walks of life.

—**J.M. Mehta**
J-186, Saket, New Delhi

Contents

1.
Abraham Lincoln

Abraham Lincoln is considered as the greatest President of the U.S.A. Besides his several other achievements, he is also remembered for his definition of democracy as 'The Government of the people, by the people and for the people.'

His Compassion

Once, Lincoln was going in a car, well dressed, to attend a meeting. On the way, he saw a pig drowning in a muddy pool. He asked the driver to stop the car, came out and without caring for his dress, entered the pool and saved the pig. In this act, he spoiled his clothes but saved a life. He did so out of compassion.

Sense of Humour

One day, Abraham Lincoln was polishing his shoes. A friend who came to meet him saw him doing so, said: "You are such a big person. Why are you polishing your own shoes?"

Lincoln smiled and said: "Then tell me, should I polish shoes of other people!"

This showed his sense of humour and great humility.

Niagara Falls

A friend asked Abraham Lincoln about his deepest impression upon seeing the Niagara Falls, the greatest natural wonder.

Lincoln replied, "The thought that struck me when I saw the Falls was – where in the world did all the water come from?"

Hold My Hand

During the Civil War in America, President Lincoln would often visit the hospitals to see the wounded soldiers.

During one such visit, the doctor pointed towards a young soldier who was about to die. Lincoln went to him and asked: "Is there anything I can do for you?"

The soldier could not recognise the President and said, "Will you write a letter to my mother?" The President himself wrote the letter as dictated by the soldier. At the end of the letter, the President had written this – Written for your son by Abraham Lincoln.

When the soldier read this, he asked: "Are you really the President?"

Lincoln replied, "Yes, I am. Is there anything else I could do?"

The soldier said, "Would you please hold my hand, it will help me to go through the end."

The President did as requested and spoke words of solace and encouragement. The soldier died peacefully.

What an act of kind compassion by the great President!

OOO

2.
Akbar

Akbar And The Hermit

At the time of the reign of king Akbar, a holy man lived in a forest and many people visited him. The hermit wanted to entertain his visitors, but had no money. So he went to Akbar for help.

When he entered the palace, he found Akbar in a prayer and overheard the king asking God to give him more wealth and power. Hearing this, the hermit was about to leave when the king saw him and asked the reason for his coming and leaving soon, without saying anything.

The hermit said: 'O king, I came to you to seek some money for entertaining my visitors. But here I found that you too are begging from God. So I thought: "What can I get from a beggar? I will now beg from God." Saying this he went away.

God is the real giver of all things.

Akbar And Birbal

King Akbar always looked for opportunities to make fun of Birbal. With this aim, he wanted to call Birbal's father, who was old and illiterate. Birbal saw through

Akbar's game plan and advised his father not to reply to any of the king's questions.

His father agreed and gave no reply to Akbar's questions. At this Akbar asked Birbal: "Is your father a fool?"

Birbal now saw an opportunity to make fun of Akbar and said: "No my Lord. My father is not a fool but he does not reply to foolish questions!"

Akbar And Birbal

The great king Akbar often used to make fun of his minister Birbal who was very wise and would pay back in the same coin.

Once they were sitting together and Akbar said: "Birbal, last night I had a strange dream. As we were walking together in the forest, we both fell in two pits, separately. Somehow we came out and then I saw that you were all full of dirt, while I was full of honey all over the body," saying this, Akbar laughed heartily.

Birbal thought for a while and then responded: "O great king, I too had a dream last night and it was almost the same as yours, but I saw something more."

Akbar was astonished and asked, "Tell me Birbal, what did you see?"

Birbal said, "If you pardon me, only then I will say." Akbar allowed him to go ahead.

Then Birbal said: "When I came out, it was exactly the same as you said. You were smeared with honey and I with dirt. What happened next I will tell you now. I started licking you and Your Majesty started licking me!"

After saying this, it was now Birbal's turn to laugh!

OOO

3.
Albert Einstein

Albert Einstein, Wife And Servant

Einstein's wife complained to him about the servant, saying he was insolent, a shirker and fool, etc. Einstein said "O.K. I will see."

Later, he called the servant and enquired from him. The servant said, "Madam was impatient, unreasonable, and bad-tempered." Einstein said, "O.K. I will see."

At this, his wife remarked, "What type of scientist are you? You have said O.K. to both me and the servant."

Einstein replied, "Both of you are right, O.K."

The Genius

Once Einstein was travelling in a train. A ticket collector came to check. Einstein looked in his pocket for the ticket but could not find it as he had left it at home. The ticket collector, knowing that he was a very very important person, said: "It is O.K. if you have left it at home."

Einstein said: "No, it is not O.K. Without the ticket I do not know my destination!"

Absent Minded

Albert Einstein was so absent minded (or so absorbed in his work) that he once used a cheque worth $1500 as a book mark, and then lost the book and also the cheque!

Telephone Number

Einstein was once asked by somebody for his telephone number. He said: "I will have to look up in the directory. I never bother to memorise information that I can find elsewhere!"

4. Alexander The Great

Opportunity

Alexander the Great visited the studio of a sculptor in Athens and found it full of statues. There he saw a statue with the face covered and its feet having wings, and enquired, "What is its name?"

The sculptor replied, 'Its name is Opportunity.'

Alexander asked, "Why is its face covered?"

The sculptor said, "Because people rarely see opportunity when it passes before them."

"But why do the feet have wings?" asked Alexander.

The sculptor replied, "Because once it flies, it won't come back."

That is why the saying 'Lost opportunity does not come back.'

You have to grab the opportunity and make the best use of it.

And The Yogi

Before invading India, Alexander had heard a lot about the spiritual heritage of India, yogis and saints. After winning battles, when Alexander was about to return to his country, he was advised to visit a popular yogi, who lived and meditated in a forest, all alone.

Alexander went to the yogi and asked him to accompany him to his country, promising him lots of wealth, honour and comforts.

The yogi refused his offer and said, "I do not need your wealth or anything else from you. I am very happy here."

Alexander went away, very much surprised and impressed.

A person truly devoted to God does not need anything from anybody, not even from a great king like Alexander!

Alexander And King Porus

When Alexander invaded India, he had to fight king Porus, who was a brave fighter and had a powerful army. Alexander defeated Porus after a fierce fight. After the battle, Porus was brought before Alexander, who enquired from him as to what treatment should be given to him. Alexander thought that Porus would beg for mercy. But Porus, being a brave and fearless warrior, unhesitating replied: "You should give me the same treatment as one king should give to another king."

This brave and straightforward answer of king Porus pleased Alexander, who admired his courage and fearlessness.

Empty Hands

Alexander was a great warrior; he conquered several kingdoms and became a great emperor. During these wars he looted a lot of valuables, wealth and property, and amassed a great treasure. But he died at a young age after suffering from a terrible illness from which he could not recover in spite of all efforts and best treatment available to him.

Just before his death, he realised that all his wealth was of no use to him and he has to leave everything behind, after his death.

After his death and upon his previous instructions, when his coffin was being carried, while his body was covered, his both hands were spread out empty. This was to show that when he was born he came empty-handed and when he died, he went empty-handed. Thus nothing goes with a person at the time of death and all material possessions are left behind.

The moral of the story is that it is no use amassing wealth and being greedy.

ooo

5.
Alexander Fleming

Several years ago, a Scottish farmer, while working outside, heard a cry for help. He left his tools, went around and saw a terrified boy, struggling to save himself from drowning in black muck. The farmer, whose name was Fleming, saved the boy from slow and sure death.

The next day a nobleman came to Fleming and introduced himself as the father of the boy whom Fleming had saved. He wanted to reward Fleming who refused to accept any payment.

At that time, Fleming's own son came to the door. The nobleman enquired about him and said to Fleming: "I will offer you a deal. Let me educate your son in the same way as my own son."

This was agreed to. Fleming's son got the best education and graduated from St.Mary's Hospital Medical School in London. Later, he became famous as the discoverer of the wonder drug 'Penicillin'.

This medicine later saved the life of the same nobleman's son when he was stricken with pneumonia.

A good deed brings its own reward.

OOO

6. Aristotle

Hurry. Do Not Be Late

A young woman approached Aristotle, one of the greatest philosophers of the world, and said to him: "Please advise, when should I start training my child?"

Aristotle asked her: "What is the age of your child?"

The woman replied: "My son is five years old."

At this, the philosopher remarked, "Then you better hurry home. You are already five years late!"

OOO

7. Guru Arjun Dev

Simplicity

Arjun Dev was a simple disciple who devoted his life to the service of his guru. He was always busy in the community kitchen, cleaning the large brass vessels and doing other odd jobs, while others spent time sitting with the Guru, discussing philosophical matters.

One day the Guru was nearing his end. All the distinguished disciples gathered around the Guru except Arjun Dev who was serving in the community kitchen. The Guru sent for him to come at once. As he entered the room breathless and still covered in black ash, all the disciples moved aside to avoid getting soiled. But the Guru was very much pleased to see him. He then declared before the entire assembly that Arjun Dev was his chosen successor.

At this the distinguish scholars began questioning: "What has he attained that we have not!"

The Guru replied, "His attainment is that he has no attainment. Therefore, he is completely open to me."

Thus, Arjun Dev became the 5th Guru. It was he who compiled the *Guru Granth Sahib*.

Supreme Sacrifice

Guru Arjun Dev attained martyrdom after imprisonment and extreme torture. He embodied love, humility and service and was very popular with the masses.

Emperor Jehangir got alarmed at the great and growing influence of the Guru. Thousands of Hindus and even some Muslims were fascinated by his simplicity and teachings. Jehangir wanted to stop this and wished to bring the Guru into the fold of Islam. When his son Khusro rebelled, he (Khusro) met the Guru and sought his blessings. This annoyed the king who fined the Guru heavily. Refusing to pay, the Guru was arrested and put in prison.

Guru Arjun Dev was tortured, seated on red-hot iron plates. He was made to sit in boiling water, and burning sand was poured on him. In his agony the Guru would say: 'Tera kiya mitha lage, Naam padarth Nanak' (whatever you ordain appears sweet. I beg for the gift of thy Name.) The Guru was then taken for a dip in the cold water of the river. Deep in meditation, the great Guru calmly passed away!

This was an act of supreme sacrifice in the annals of history.

8. King Arthur

What A Woman Wants

When young king Arthur was ambushed in a battle and imprisoned by a neighbouring king, the latter offered to free him if he answered a question, to his captor's satisfaction.

The question was: 'What do women really want?' Arthur's victor gave him a year to find the right answer; failing to do that, he would face the penalty of death.

Arthur consulted all his friends and advisors. They gave him different answers but none satisfied him. Someone advised him to consult a witch who had the right answer. The witch was consulted but she put a condition, which was agreed to.

The witch gave the answer: 'What a woman really wants is to be able to be incharge of her own life.'

This was the right answer and Arthur's life was saved.

OOO

9.
Baba Farid

God Is The Real Support

One day Baba Farid, the great Sufi saint, was standing with the support of his staff. Suddenly, he threw his staff and turned pale! People asked him "What happened?"

Baba Farid replied: "As I was standing God said to me: 'Farid, why do you need the support of the staff when I am with you?' When I heard this, the staff fell down and I turned pale, in awe of the Lord."

Indeed, God is the real support we need.

OOO

10. B.G. Tilak

B.G. Tilak was one of India's greatest leaders. He gave the slogan 'Self-rule is my birthright.' He had great love for books, as shown in the following anecdote.

Value Of Books

Tilak was about to be married. His father-in-law wanted to give him a precious gift in accordance with the prevailing marriage customs. When Tilak came to know about this, he sent a message to his father-in-law saying: 'I do not need any valuable article as a marriage gift. I do not desire gold, any vehicle, costly clothing or watch, etc. In case you really want to give me something then please give me some useful books which may prove helpful in my present and future life.'

His father-in-law followed his advice. This shows the great love of Tilak for learning and knowledge.

OOO

11.
George Bernard Shaw

Pungent Humour

A man continued talking to G.B. Shaw, much against his wishes. The man wanted to impress Shaw with his knowledge but the latter was not interested.

Shaw got fed up and said: "It seems between the two of us, we know all that is to be known."

The man asked, surprised, "How is that?"

Shaw replied "You seem to know everything except that you are a big BORE and I know that!"

Good Books

As a youth G.B. Shaw was fond of dancing and merry-making in the company of his friends. His father wanted to advise him and said: "I do not feel bad about spending your time with friends dancing and singing, as I want you to enjoy life. But also make some new friends, who may be your life-long companions and guides. On the basis of my experience, I can tell you that you cannot find better friends than good books."

Shaw followed the advice and rose to become a great writer.

Wit Of Shaw

G.B. Shaw was greatly admired for his wit, wisdom and literary talent, but he was not good-looking.

A lady admirer of Shaw was very attractive and beautiful. She wanted to marry Shaw and wrote to him: 'Look, I have beauty and you have intellect and wisdom. If we marry, our offspring will inherit my beauty and your wisdom. So please accept my proposal of marriage.'

Shaw was not impressed and he did not want to marry. So he replied: 'Imagine what will happen if such children inherit my ugliness and your lack of wisdom!'

The lady got the message.

OOO

12.
Lord Buddha

Abuses Not Accepted

One day, when Lord Buddha was sitting in a meditative pose, a man came near him and went on abusing him for a long time, till he exhausted himself. Meanwhile Lord Buddha just sat calmly, undisturbed.

When the man became quiet Buddha asked him: 'My friend, tell me, if someone gives you something and you don't take it, then with whom does that thing remain?'

The man laughed and said: "You ask me a foolish question. Obviously that will remain with the giver. You don't know even this simple answer."

Buddha smiled and said: "In that case, I don't accept the abuses which you had given to me!"

The man felt ashamed and fell at Lord Buddha's feet.

The Secret Of Peace

Once Lord Buddha was sitting surrounded by his disciples. A prince was also sitting nearby. The faces of disciples reflected peace and glow of cheerfulness, while the prince looked sad and gloomy.

A learned visitor to the Lord noted this difference and asked Buddha: 'Sir, inspite of their hard life your disciples are full of peace and delight, while the prince to whom all the facilities and comforts are available, looks sad and without cheer. Please enlighten me, why is this so?'

Buddha smiled and said. 'This is because my disciples keep evenness of mind and their mental peace is not disturbed by any happening. They do not brood over the past or worry about the future. They always live in the present and move with the present. This is the secret of their peace and cheerfulness.'

What a practical lesson for all!

Buddha And The Robber

A strong and ferocious robber murdered people and cut their fingers to make a garland to put around his neck. Once, in a forest he saw a monk walking towards his hut. The robber warned him not to come further, otherwise he would murder him. The monk was Lord Buddha and he continued walking towards the robber who was brandishing his sword. On reaching near him Buddha said: 'Are you very strong?'

The robber replied: 'Yes, no doubt.'

Then Buddha asked: 'Can you break the branch of that tree?'

The robber easily broke the branch.

Buddha then said: 'Now join that branch with the tree, as before.'

The robber was unable to do that and was helpless. He got instant wisdom and fell at the feet of Buddha and became his disciple. That robber was Angulimal.

Food Or Sermon

A Buddhist preacher was giving sermon to a beggar who was hardly paying any attention. The preacher got fed up and complained to Lord Buddha who called for the beggar, saying: 'I shall myself give sermon to him.' When the beggar came, Buddha asked another disciple to take him away and give food. The beggar was given food.

At this the first disciple asked: 'Lord, but you have not given any sermon to him.'

Lord Buddha said: 'Son, just now he needs food. I shall give him sermon tomorrow.'

13. Chanakya

How He Loved His Mother

Chanakya was born in an ordinary family. He lost his father when he was an infant. So he was brought up by his loving mother, with great care, caution and wisdom. Chanakya loved and respected his mother very much. He had a rare category of healthy teeth and his mother told him that such teeth belonged to kings. She predicted that one day he would become a great king and then he might forget her.

When Chanakya heard this from his mother whom he adored, he felt hurt. He went out and broke his front tooth with a stone and told his mother that he would prefer not to be a king, so that he does not forget his mother.

Chanakya had such an exceptional and amazing adoration for his mother!

Chanakya And Thief

Chanakya, who is famous for making Chandragupt Maurya a great king, is said to have lived a life of austerity. Even though he became his Prime Minister, he used to live in a hut and did not have much material possessions except for his bare requirements.

One day a thief barged into his hut and found Chanakya sleeping on a wooden cot in one corner, covered with an old worn-out blanket. The thief could not find any valuables around Chanakya. But as he was about to go, he noticed a heap of new blankets in another corner of the hut. As he tried to lift a few and run away, he was caught by some watchmen and brought before Chanakya.

The thief admitted his crime but asked Chanakya: 'Sir, I wonder, despite new blankets lying in the room, why had you covered your body with an old worn-out blanket in this bitter cold?'

Chanakya told him that those blankets were meant for distribution to the destitute and he had no right to use them. That is why he was using the blanket which belonged to him.

Such was the spirit of service and selflessness of one of the greatest sons of India.

14. Confucius

Good Governance

Confucius was a great philosopher of China. One day, he and his disciples were trekking across a mountainous region when they came across a woman weeping beside a grave.

Confucius enquired: 'Whom are you mourning?'

The woman sobbed and said: 'My only son, who was mauled by the tiger. His father and grandfather also died the same way.'

Confucius then asked: 'In that case why don't you leave this place?'

She replied: 'Here the government is not oppressive.'

Confucius then pointed out to his disciples: 'Take note, an oppressive government is more dangerous than marauding tigers.' And they resumed their journey.

The Last Teaching

During his last moments of life, the great Chinese philosopher Confucius said to his disciple: 'Son, look into my mouth and check if there is tongue inside.'

The disciple said: 'Master, yes, the tongue is there inside the mouth.'

Then the master asked: 'Look again and see whether there are teeth inside?'

The disciple said: 'Master, there is none.'

The master said: 'The tongue was born first and it is still there intact, but the teeth which were born later are missing. Why have they gone earlier?' Hearing this, the disciples were all silent and surprised and looked towards the master who said: 'Look, the tongue is soft, therefore it is still there. The teeth were hard, hence they broke away.'

This was the last teaching of the great master.

15. C.V. Raman

Born Without A Spoon!

Someone asked the famous Indian scientist Sir C.V. Raman: 'Sir, were you born with a silver spoon in your mouth?'

He replied: 'I was born without any spoon in my mouth, because at the time of my birth, my father got a monthly salary of rupees ten only!'

Perhaps, this humble start was the cause of his great scientific discoveries.

OOO

16.
Carl Jung

Pain Is Good For Us

Carl Jung, the renowned psychiatrist, once said that when people approached him with stories of personal pain, he would smile and say: 'Something good will come out of it.'

We human beings need to know, recognise, understand and accept the fact that pain is an essential adjunct of our life and is actually good for us. We all grow from experiencing pain and therefore should have a positive attitude towards it.

Remember the saying: 'No pain, no gain!'

OOO

17. Thomas Alva Edison

Great Inventor

Edison is considered the greatest inventor of the world for all times. It is said that on his wedding day, he excused himself as he had to attend to some very important work which needed his urgent attention.

When he was not seen for a long time, his close relatives started looking for him. Several hours later he was found, so completely engrossed in his scientific experiments that he forgot that he was married just that day. How interesting!

Great Genius

Edison believed in 'Keep Trying.' He stated that a genius was 97% plain hard work. He demonstrated that himself by making 1700 unsuccessful trials before he came up with a new product. He made over 1000 experiments before he succeeded in inventing the electric bulb.

By his numerous inventions, he enriched human life and happiness. He said 'I will never invent anything which with destroy life.' He was a great man as well as scientist.

Cleanliness And Devotion

From his childhood Edison wanted to be a scientist but poverty stood in the way. His mother, seeing her son's great ambition, took him to a scientist. The scientist wanted to test him so he gave Edison a broom and asked him to clean his laboratory. Edison cleaned it very nicely and remained engrossed in his work. He put everything in place.

The scientist was greatly impressed and said to his mother: 'Please leave him with me. He will become a great scientist one day, because he has the required qualities.'

And later Edison became the world's greatest inventor.

18. M.K. Gandhi

Advice To A Student

To a student going abroad for studies, Gandhiji gave advice as follows:-

Speak little. Listen to everyone, but do only what is right.

Keep account of every minute and do each piece of work, when it should be done.

Live like the poor. Never take pride in riches. Keep account of every pie (paisa) you spend.

Study with concentration.Take regular exercise. Eat sparingly.

Maintain a daily diary.

Gandhiji And III Class

Gandhiji used to travel in train by III class. Once, someone enquired: 'Bapu, why do you travel by III class?'

Gandhiji replied: 'Because there is no IV class!'

He was such a ready wit and humble person.

Gandhiji And Khan Abdul Ghaffar Khan

Gandhiji used to gently slap a child whom he loved. One day Khan Abdul Ghaffar Khan noticed this and said to Gandhiji: 'Bapu, you slap the one you love, but you have never slapped me. This means you do not love me.'

Gandhiji looked at the huge body of Ghaffar Khan and said: 'I do love you but I do not slap you because if you return in the same coin, then I will be crushed.' All around had a good laugh.

The Gita And The Bible

An Englishman came to Gandhiji and said: 'I have read the Bhagavad Gita and like it.'

Gandhiji responded by saying: 'I like it too.'

The man added that he liked the Gita better than the Bible.

Gandhiji said: 'I read the Bible and like it too.'

The Englishman then said: 'Since I find the Gita better than the Bible, I would like to convert to Hinduism.'

Gandhiji thought a while and said: 'I think you have not understood the Bible well. Since you are not a good Christian, how can you be a good Hindu?

It is therefore better that you first become a good Christian. If you succeed in doing this, you will become a good human being. And if you do so, then you will not only be a good Christian, but a good Hindu, a good Muslim and a good Jew as well. The walls of narrow, separate religions within your heart will then break away.'

This shows Gandhiji's understanding of true religion, unity of all religions and his broad-mindedness.

Barber Without Tools

Once Gandhiji was travelling in a train to Calcutta (Kolkata). He dictated a letter to his staff member and wanted to get it typed before the train reached a particular station on the way, as it was to be delivered to someone there. His staff told him that he had not brought the typewriter.

Another leader would have flown into a rage, but Gandhiji simply said: 'Whom I call a barber, I expect him to come with tools.'

This shows Gandhiji's humour as well as tact and patience.

Mahapurush Without Ticket

On another occasion, Gandhiji was travelling with his staff members. Before the train moved from the station, Gandhiji came to know that they were all without tickets. He summoned the station master who said: 'Mahapurush like you do not need tickets.'

Gandhiji said: 'Is this how you allow so many 'mahapurush' to travel without tickets?' The tickets were then purchased for all.

Compare this with the politicians of today who want so many concessions and extra privileges for themselves and their cronies!

In Champaran

It was difficult to meet women in Champaran. Gandhiji deputed Kasturba and her associates to meet the women who would not even open their doors.

At sunset, Kasturba knocked at one home and said: "We are tired and thirsty, please give us a glass of water." At this, a door was slightly opened and a woman's hand came out holding a glass of water. Kasturba drank the water and said: "We have seen your hand but we want to see the woman behind this hand."

The woman inside broke down and said: "We are three woman in this house and we all share only one untorn saree. As one woman has gone out wearing that saree, how can we open the door and expose our semi-naked bodies?" Upon hearing this Kasturba said: 'Close this door, the doors of your heart are open.'

When Kasturba returned to Gandhiji, she told him the heart-rending story of the plight of women in Champaran. Gandhiji then resolved to work for the upliftment of the women there.

Charity

Mahatma Gandhi travelled from place to place to collect funds for the Charkha Sangh. During his tour, once he was addressing a meeting in a town in Orissa. In response to his appeal, people donated money. One poor old woman also came to Gandhiji to offer her donation. She brought out a copper coin from the folds of her old saree and gave it to Gandhiji, who took the coin and kept it very carefully.

Jamnalal Bajaj, an associate of Gandhiji who was keeping all donations, asked for the coin from Gandhiji who refused to part with it, and said: 'If a man has several lakhs and gives away a few thousands, it does not mean much. But this coin was all that the poor woman had. And she gave me all that she possessed. What a great sacrifice she has made!'

Death Of A Hero

In 1933, Gandhiji was released after he undertook a fast in Jail. He said to his colleague Anand: 'I did not expect to be released and thought I should be allowed to die. In fact, I had prepared myself for such an eventuality and even given away my personal things to nurses and other attendants. I do not know how my death by fasting would have been regarded by people.'

Anand answered: 'It would have been a most glorious death.'

Bapu said: 'Nonsense. Where is the glory in it? But do you know, it is written in my horoscope that I have to die a heroic death.'

Anand said: 'But Bapu, even death by fasting is a heroic death; it means courage of the highest order.'

Gandhiji remarked: 'No. I do not think so. My death is to come about either on the gallows or by shooting. And that indeed would be a truly heroic death. Not one by fasting in bed.'

How true was Gandhiji's prediction!

Gandhiji And Zero Marks

Gandhiji was in prison in the Aga Khan Palace, when his birthday was approaching on 2nd October. His fellow prisoners decided to play a game with him. Each member was given passages from the speeches of great thinkers and leaders and was asked to discover the author. Three passages were given to Gandhiji and his answers were all wrong, so he was given zero marks. Later it was revealed that all the three passages were from speeches made by Gandhiji himself. Gandhiji joined in the laughter with all around.

Minus Four

While in Scotland, Gandhiji visited one of the dairies. He asked a Scot what he called the dress he was wearing.

He replied: 'Plus four' as he was heavily dressed.

Then the Scot asked Gandhiji: 'What do you call what you are wearing?'

Gandhiji replied: 'Minus four.'

Gandhiji was wearing only a dhoti and was wrapped in a shawl.

Stickler For Time

Mahatma Gandhi was a great stickler for time. Once a professor fixed an appointment to meet him at 11.00 a.m. at his Wardha ashram. The professor reached the ashram at 10.45 a.m. and saw a man sweeping the front courtyard.

He told the man: 'Go and tell Gandhiji that Professor has come to meet him.'

The man said: 'Gandhi will see you at 11.00 a.m.'

The professor said: 'But you should go and tell him about my arrival.'

The man did not go and repeated: 'I have told you, Gandhi will come and meet you at 11.00 a.m.'

The professor waited. At 11.00 a.m. the same man stood before him and said: 'I have come to meet you at 11.00 a.m. I am Gandhi.'

The professor was greatly surprised to see that the great man was sweeping his yard himself. This showed the sense of punctuality and the dignity of labour of Mahatma Gandhi.

Three Monkeys Of Gandhiji

It is said that Gandhiji used to keep small statues of three monkeys in his room. These monkeys were a source of amusement and surprise to the visitors. Gandhi had kept them with a purpose in mind as there was something special in the posture of these statues. One monkey kept his eyes covered with both hands. The second monkey had his ears covered with both hands, while the third monkey kept his mouth shut with his hand.

These monkeys conveyed the following message for all to follow:-

Do not see any evil
Do not hear any evil
Do not speak any evil.

Fooling The Mahatma

Dr. C.V. Raman, the renowned physicist, while he was Professor at Calcutta University invited Mahatma Gandhi for dinner when the latter was on a visit. To entertain his distinguished guest, he demonstrated some experiments based on principles of sound. He also explained the intricate theories which were beyond Gandhiji to follow. However, Gandhiji went on nodding in appreciation.

Suddenly Raman realised that Gandhiji could not understand the intricate theories. At that point he stopped his experiments and said: 'I am a fool who is explaining all this to you, and you are a greater fool who is nodding without understanding.'

In all humility, Gandhiji just smiled.

He Looks Like A Sparrow

During his visit to Punjab, a meeting was arranged to welcome Gandhiji at Amritsar. A large gathering of people had collected and there was great rush as everyone wanted to see Gandhiji who was seated at the centrestage among other dignitaries.

Two burly stout Punjabi farmers with their large sticks in hand were pushing towards the stage as they also wished to see the big man of India.

When they reached near the stage, they enquired from a volunteer: 'Where is Gandhiji?'

The man pointed towards a thin, meek looking person dressed in a dhoti.

Seeing him one remarked to the other: 'Oh, we were told that he was a 'very big man.' That is why we came to see him. He looks like a sparrow!'

Saying this, they turned back.

These illiterate persons thought in terms of physical size and not the stature of Gandhiji!

Humour Of Gandhiji

G.K. Gokhale was one of the founding fathers of India's freedom movement. He founded the 'Servants of India' Society.

Gokhale was greatly influenced by his guide and leader, M.G. Ranade. Before his death, Ranade had gifted a scarf to Gokhale and the latter kept it very carefully with love and respect. Several years later, when Gokhale was in South Africa with Gandhiji, he was invited to attend a function. Gokhale wanted to wear that scarf which required ironing. Gandhiji offered his help for this work.

At this Gokhale remarked: 'I can trust you as a lawyer but not as a washer man! If you spoiled this scarf, how sad it would be. You do not know how dearly I cherish this scarf!'

But Gandhiji was also resolute and he did a good job and proved his reliability.

Ready Wit

When Gandhiji went to the England to attend the Round Table Conference, he met King George V at a reception.

When he came out of the palace, a reporter asked him 'Mr.Gandhi, what did the king say about your dress?'

Gandhiji was scantily dressed in a dhoti, etc.

He replied: His Majesty did not make any comment. After all, he was wearing enough for the two of us.'

Gandhiji was a ready wit.

Gandhiji's Tact

Once somebody asked Gandhiji 'Is the Ramayana true or false?'

It was a strange question. Gandhiji thought for a while and said: 'When the Ramayana was written, I was not there!'

Gandhiji And His Critic

A critic of Gandhiji wrote a nasty poem on him and appended a note saying: 'Mr. Gandhi, you will find it useful.'

Gandhiji read it, removed the pin attached to it and returned the papers to the man, saying: "Yes, I have retained the useful item."

OOO

19. Guru Nanak

Prayer

A Muslim priest once asked Guru Nanak to come with him and pray to Allah in a mosque. As Guru Nanak believed in one God and spoke of the same faith for all, he agreed to go with the priest. While the mullah knelt down for prayer and put his fingers into his ears, Guru Nanak remained standing in silence.

So the mullah taunted the Guru and said: 'Why don't you pray like me and why are you just standing?'

The Guru smiled and said: 'While you were uttering some holy words with your lips, your mind was roaming elsewhere in your stables and thinking of horses.'

The mullah felt ashamed and astonished.

Prayer should be sincere and with full devotion in God, otherwise it becomes a useless ritual.

Guru Nanak And A Rich Merchant

A rich merchant was a devotee of Guru Nanak. But he was very proud of his wealth and amassed lakhs of rupees. The Guru wanted to enlighten him by teaching a lesson.

One day Guru Nanak said to him: 'I am giving you this

needle for safe custody. Please return it to me when we meet in the next life.'

The merchant took the needle, without realising the true meaning of what the Guru said.

Later on, he realised that he cannot take the needle to his next life. Nothing goes with him when a man dies; everything is left behind. So he came to the Guru, returned the needle saying: 'Guruji, how can I take the needle to my next life?'

Guru Nanak smiled and said: 'If you can't take this small needle with you after death, then how can you take the millions which you have amassed?

The merchant learnt his lesson.

Guru Nanak And The Elephant

Once Guru Nanak was walking along the riverside and found that an elephant was lying unconscious on the sand, and his keeper was weeping over it as he thought the elephant was dead. Guruji came to him, saw the elephant and told the keeper to pour cold water from the river over his head. He did so and the elephant recovered after some time.

The keeper thought that his elephant became alive due to the miracle of Guruji. Guru Nanak told him that the elephant had become unconscious due to heat and so it fell down. When cold water was poured over his head, the effect of heat was nullified and the elephant recovered.

We should first try to know the reason for our problem and then try to find the proper remedy.

Guru Nanak And Holy Men

Guru Nanak went to a village where there were plenty of holy men living already.

They sent him a glass full of milk, giving a message that while they respected him, the place was already full of holy men and therefore he was not needed.

The Guru understood well and responded by placing a flower over the milk-filled glass. This sent a message that he would remain like a flower. The other holy men were much impressed and showed respect to the Guru and welcomed him.

20. Isaac Newton

Like A Child

When Newton lay dying, a friend said to him: 'It must be a source of pride and gratification to know that you penetrated so deeply into the knowledge of Nature's laws.'

Newton humbly said: 'Far from being proud, I feel like a little child who has found a few bright coloured shells and pebbles while the vast ocean of Truth stretches unknown and unexplored before my eager fingers.'

Such was the humility and absence of any false pride of a great scientist of his time.

OOO

21. Ishwar Chandra Vidyasagar

Vidyasagar was a highly educated and enlightened person of Bengal. At the same time, he was a man of great humility and compassion.

Compassion and Humility

One day, as he was passing through the marketplace, he came across an old poor labourer who was going with a heavy load on his back and walking with unsteady steps.

Vidyasagar felt great pity for him and with a view to helping him, carried the load to his destination and also gave him some money. The labourer did not recognise him but blessed him, expressed his gratitude and felt happy.

A kind and good-hearted person feels happy by giving something and also makes the receiver happy.

There is happiness in giving and helping others.

OOO

22.
J.L. Nehru

Beautiful Moments

Once a person asked Nehru: 'In whose arms did you spend the most beautiful moments of your life?' It was a strange question but Nehruji calmly said: 'In the arms of another man's wife!' Hearing this answer everyone around was surprised!

Nehru smiled and said: 'She was my dear mother.'

Drinking Blood

Moti Lal Nehru, father of J.L. Nehru was bred in Western culture and was fond of Western dress and food. One day, he was drinking some red wine. Jawahar Lal, who was then a child, saw this and rushed inside to tell his mother that father was drinking 'blood.'

Love For Children

Nehru was very fond of children who also loved him. Once, a child asked Nehru: 'Chachaji, what was your most and least weight, and when?'

Nehru was a ready wit. He instantly replied: 'When I was in Ahmed Nagar Jail, my weight was 162 pounds. And my least weight was 7.5 pounds, when I was born!'

Hearing this all children burst into laughter and Nehru enjoyed their merriment.

OOO

23.
J.C. Bose

Self Respect

J.C. Bose, the renowned Indian scientist, after completing higher studies in science in the U.K. returned to India and was appointed a Professor in Science in a University where another English professor having equal qualifications was also teaching science. At that time India was under the British rule.

After a month when J.C. Bose got his salary, he found that he got less than his English counterpart. So he protested to the University authorities who did not listen to him. At this, Bose thought that as it was insulting to accept lower salary, he would teach without accepting that salary. The University did not care and Bose continued teaching for free. His method of teaching was so inspiring and brilliant that more and more students flocked to his classes. This continued for three years after which the University realised their mistake and accepted his rightful demand of higher salary. He was also given arrears of salary for three years and was accorded the honour due to him.

In this way, J.C. Bose set an example of how to safeguard personal self respect and sense of honour.

OOO

24. King Janak

How To Avoid Bad Habits

King Janak had acquired true knowledge through long practice of dedication and devotion.

Once, a man came to seek his advice on how to control anger. Janak listened to him and realised his problem; he went to a pillar, put both his hands around it and encircled it tightly, and started shouting: 'Please help me! The pillar has caught me and it is not leaving me!'

The man who had come to seek his advice laughed and said: 'O king, the pillar has not caught you but you have caught it. So you have to leave the pillar yourself.'

The king replied: 'That is what you have to do. You have to leave anger. It is you who have caught anger; it will go away if you do not catch it.' The man became wiser and resolved to follow the king's advice.

This is how we can shun bad habits by keeping away from them. In case we have acquired any, we have to leave them with full determination.

Lesson For A King

Once king Janak was passing through a city. His servants were stopping the people and moving them away to facilitate the smooth travel of the king. This was causing much inconvenience to the common folk.

By chance, Rishi Ashtavakra, the renowned saint of that time, who was also passing that way refused to get away. The servants arrested him and brought before the king. When the king came to know the whole story, he was very much impressed by the saint who had earlier told the king's servant that it was improper for a king to put his subjects to inconvenience for his own comfort and convenience.

Ashtavakra also said: 'It is my duty as a holy man to give right advice to the king.'

King Janak admired the courage and the correct thinking of the rishi. He sought forgiveness of the saint and honoured him by accepting him as his 'Raj Guru.'

25. Lord Krishna

Honour Of Draupadi

Having lost everything, including himself, brothers and Draupadi in a gambling bout, Yudhishtra and his brothers were helpless when Duhshasan was eager to strip Draupadi naked, in the court of Duryodhana. They could do nothing as they were slaves of Duryodhana.

Then Draupadi turned to Lord Krishna for help. She cried out to Krishna: 'But for thee, none else can come to my rescue.' It is said that Shri Krishna appeared and said to her: 'Draupadi, can you tell me if at any time you have given a single piece of cloth to some one in need?' Darupadi recalled that one day she was standing on a river bank when a sanyasi was taking bath. A sudden and swift wave of water swept away the single loin cloth worn by sanyasi, leaving him naked.

Darupadi saw this and at once tore a piece of cloth from her saree, gave it to the sanyasi and thus helped him to come out of the river.

This incident gave Lord Krishna a starting point to save her honour. He drew out several lengths of material to Draupadi, out of that piece of cloth she had given to the sanyasi. Duhshasan, therefore, could not strip her naked when Lord Krishna was there to help her.

OOO

26.
Lal Bahadur Shastri

Help And Kindness

Lal Bahadur Shastri was then Railway Minister and was travelling in a train. His seat was reserved in a first class compartment. But he also had an ailing companion whose seat was in the III class compartment. Shastriji put his ailing companion in first class seat and himself went to III class compartment and went to sleep, covering himself with a sheet.

A ticket collector came. He did not recognise Shastriji, so he admonished him for occupying a wrong seat. But when he came to know of Shastriji's identity, he was surprised and out of fear said: 'Sir, let me escort you to the first class compartment.'

But Shastriji said: 'Please don't bother me and let me sleep here.'

Later on, the ticket collector investigated the matter and came to know the whole secret.

How kind and compassionate was Shastriji!

Do Not Accept The Job

Lal Bahadur Shastri, a former Prime Minister of India, was a man of great integrity. He would never accept any undue favour. When he was Prime Minister, a big company offered a good job with a handsome salary to his son, for which he sought his father's permission.

When Shastriji saw the appointment letter he told his son: 'This job is being offered to you because you are the son of the Prime Minister, and not on your merit. If you accept the job, it will indirectly be a bribe to me. So do not accept this job.'

This was an example of great integrity of a great man.

Child In A Basket

When L.B. Shastri was an infant, his mother took him to Varanasi for a bath in the river Ganges. There was very large crowd and due to the pushing and jostling the child fell from the lap of the mother. Due the rush, the mother could not find the son in spite of her best efforts. She went home full of sorrow. Everyone in the home was sad and disappointed. Later on, a policeman came to them with an infant. In the rush of the crowd, when the child fell, he fell in the basket of a farmer and was thus safe and sound!

27.
Lord Mahavira

I Am The King

Once, Lord Mahavira was passing over a sandy path, where he left his footmarks. An astrologer saw these and guessed them to be the footmarks of a great king. Out of curiosity, he followed those marks and soon he saw Mahavira standing.

He enquired whether he was a king, to which Mahavira replied. 'Yes, I am the king.'

The astrologer asked: 'But where is your army?' Lord said: 'I do not need army, as I have no enemy.'

The man asked: 'But you have no kingdom.'

Mahavira said: 'My body is my kingdom. I am king of my body and mind. I am king of myself.'

Lord Mahavira had attained a state where he did not need any material objects, kingdom or army. He was the real king.

OOO

28.
Mirza Ghalib

Mirza Ghalib And Mangoes

Mirza Ghalib was very fond of mangoes. During the season, he enjoyed eating the fruit in the company of his friends and admirers.

One day he was eating mangoes along with his companions, sitting in front of his haveli. They were all throwing the peels and the seeds in one corner of the street. As they were enjoying the fruit, a donkey passed by, sniffed at the peels and the seeds and without eating anything went away.

A rival poet of Mirza Ghalib who also happened to pass that way at that very moment saw the donkey turning away from the pile of peels.

This man did not like mangoes. He hailed Ghalib and said in a sarcastic manner: 'Look Mirza, even a donkey does not eat mangoes which you relish so much!

Mirza Ghalib prompted responded: 'Yes, only donkeys do not eat mangoes.'

Everyone laughed and the rival poet went away much annoyed.

OOO

29.
Mullah Nasruddin

Secret Of Happiness

Mullah Nasruddin, a medieval Sufi master was famous for strange methods of teaching his disciples. Once, a student came from a far off place to learn the secret of happiness from the saint. With him, he had a bag of clothes and valuables for his use. The Mullah looked at him and then suddenly snatched his bag and ran away. The student also ran after him but could not catch the master who had disappeared.

The student gave up all hope and sat defeated, cursing himself for his foolish pursuit. After some time, the Mullah appeared and gave back the bag to the student and said: 'Here is your happiness. Have you found it now?'

The student said: 'Yes, I am happy now.'

The Mullah then said: 'Were you not happy before, when you had the bag? Will you now continue to be happy when the bag remains with you?'

The question prompted the student to think and he reached the conclusion that true happiness was not connected with material possessions. The Mullah then told him that happiness and unhappiness are two different states of the same mind. If you want to be truly happy, you have to cultivate even-mindedness.

OOO

30. Napoleon Bonaparte

God Sees All

Once, a little boy was given four bananas by his father, two for himself and two for his sister.

The boy ate his bananas and kept two for his sister. His father noticed this and asked him: 'Why have you kept these two; you could have eaten these two also as nobody was seeing you.'

He said: 'These two are for sister. Had I eaten these, God would have seen. You had told me that God sees everything.'

The boy later in life became Napoleon Bonaparte, the great warrior and conqueror.

Old Debt

Napoleon spent his childhood in poverty. But he became emperor of France by dint of his hard work and courage. After he became emperor, one day, while moving around, he went to the school in front of his old house where an old woman had her shop.

Napoleon came to the old woman and said: 'Old mother, many years ago, a boy named Napoleon used to study in the nearby school. Do you remember him?'

She said: 'Yes I remember something about him. He was a very good boy, always helping others and serving the needy.'

Napoleon said: 'He used to buy some eatables from you. Does he owe you something?'

The woman said: 'No, he owed me nothing.'

Napoleon said: 'I am same Napoleon. You don't remember but I know, I had bought something from you, for which I had not paid.'

Saying this, Napoleon gave her a small purse full of coins. He repaid his old debt.

Clothing And Qualities

Once a painter came to emperor Napoleon. He was dressed in dirty worn-out clothes. Napoleon did not care for him and asked him to sit in a distant corner.

Later Napoleon called the painter and came to know that he was a master of great art and skill. After a brief conversation with the emperor, the painter asked leave to go. Napoleon got up, shook hands with him and walked some distance to see him off, as a mark of respect.

The painter was much surprised and asked the emperor: 'Sir, when I came you did not care for me, but now you are showing much courtesy when I am going away!'

Napoleon laughed and said: 'On arrival, a visitor is judged by his dress. But if he is shown respect on his departure, it is because of his qualities.'

31. Prophet Mohammed

Respect For A Human Being

Once when Prophet Mohammed was sitting somewhere in Medina, a funeral procession passed by and he stood up as a mark of respect. His followers who were also sitting beside him exclaimed that the deceased was not a Muslim, but a Jew!

The Prophet remarked 'But he was also a human being.'

All religions, in essence, teach humanism, unity, love and harmony.

OOO

32.
R.N. Tagore

Fearlessness

One day, Rabindra Nath Tagore, the great poet philosopher, was busy writing poetry. A jealous rival sent an assassin with a dagger. The killer entered the room where Tagore was sitting. Tagore continued writing poetry and motioned him to a chair. The man sat down while Tagore remained engrossed in his work paying no attention to the intruder. It looked as if Tagore forgot about the man and took no notice of him.

Some time passed like this and the man grew so bored in the absence of any attention from the poet that he walked out disgusted.

OOO

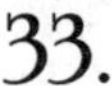

33. Dr. Rajendra Prasad

Dr. Rajendra Prasad was the first President of India. Here is an incident of his life when he was a student of a college at Calcutta. An Englishman was the principal of that college.

Self Confidence

It was the day of declaration of result of the final examination and all the students had gathered in the hall. The principal came with a list in his hand and said: 'This list contains names of successful candidates that I am going to announce. Those whose names are not announced should consider themselves as unsuccessful, but they need not feel disappointed. They should work hard and pass with distinction next year.'

When all the names in the list were announced, one student got up and said: 'Sir, you have not called out my name!'

The principal said: 'Your name is not in the list, so you have failed.'

The student said: 'This is impossible, I shall pass in First Class.'

The principal repeated, 'You are fail.'

The student insisted: 'No, it can't be so. My name has been omitted, by mistake!'

The principal got annoyed and imposed a fine of five rupees. But the student was quite adamant on his point and the principal went on increasing the fine and raised it to fifty rupees!

Meanwhile, the clerk who had prepared the list came running to the principal and said: 'Sir, the name of the student who had topped the list was omitted by mistake. Here is his name, please include it in the list.'

This was the name of the same student who was so confident of his success. The principal felt ashamed and said: 'I am very sorry, my boy. I am much pained at my mistake.'

The same student later on, after India got freedom and became republic, achieved the distinction of becoming the first President of India.

He was full of confidence and an embodiment of simple living and high thinking.

34. Ramakrishna Paramhansa

How To Live

One day Ramakrishna Paramhansa delivered the following sermon to his disciples:-

Live in the world like a maid servant in a rich man's house. She performs all the household duties, brings up the master's child and speaks to him as 'my son'. But in her heart she knows quite well that neither the house nor the child belongs to her. She performs all her duties, while her mind dwells on her native place.

Likewise, do you worldly duties but fix your mind on God. And know that house, family and son do not belong to you, they are all God's. You are only his servant.

This is the reality of life.

Learn Detachment

Ramakrishna, the great saint, used to advise his followers to practice detachment.

He would cite the example of a dry coconut. It is difficult to shell out copra from a green coconut, as it remains attached to the inner walls of the coconut.

But in a dry coconut, it is easy to get out, even without

breaking it, as it has detached itself from the hard dry shell.

Such is the advantage of detachment which gives freedom from fear, worry and even pain.

Therefore, learn and practice detachment in your daily life, in thought, word and deed.

❍❍❍

35. Maharaja Ranjit Singh

Kindness Of Maharaja

Maharaja Ranjit Singh was travelling with his retinue when a stone hit his forehead and injured him, and blood started flowing. His soldiers ran around and caught hold of an old woman who had thrown the stone, unaware of the happening. Everyone expected that she would be punished severely.

The poor old woman wept and begged for mercy. She told the Maharaja that she was very hungry and was trying to get some mangoes from the tree, by hitting it with stones. It was an unfortunate incident that the stone hit the Maharaja.

The Maharaja thought a while and said: 'Look, when the old woman hit the ordinary tree, it would give her sweet mangoes. As I am a Maharaja, it is only proper that I should give her much more.'

The Maharaja gave her money to buy food and other things.

All those present praised the Maharaja for his kindness and generosity.

Equal Treatment

Maharaja Ranjit Singh had only one good eye. The other eye was damaged and lost sight during childhood. But no one dared to call him a 'one eyed' person. Some of his detractors challenged any one to call the Maharaja so, in his presence.

A daring man, who was a poet, accepted this challenge. He composed a poem eulogising the Maharaja mentioning his noble qualities. In his composition, he mentioned the fact of the Maharaja being 'one eyed' in such a way that it pleased the king. He projected the Maharaja as a just ruler who saw all his subjects with 'one eye', which meant that he treated all in an impartial manner.

Maharaja was much pleased with the poet and rewarded him for his tact and talent.

36. Ramana Maharishi

Humour Of Ramana

Sri Ramana Maharishi's teacher visited him several years after he left school in Madurai.

Maharishi gave him a copy of his book of verses. The teacher was impressed and asked Ramana the meaning of a verse in the book.

The Maharishi laughed and pointed out to the people standing nearby and said: 'Look at my teacher. I left the school as I was bothered by his questions. Now, he has come all the way from Madurai to question me again!'

Everyone around burst into laughter to the amusement of Maharishi Ramana and his teacher.

OOO

37. Shankaracharya

From his very childhood Shankaracharya showed signs of spirituality. As a small boy he sought permission of his mother to take sanyas (renunciation) but his mother wouldn't agree. Just to please her, he did not take sanyas for the time being.

Later on, an incident changed his life. One day, while he was taking a dip in the river, a crocodile caught hold of his leg and was about to drag him away.

He cried to her mother: 'Mother, the crocodile is about to take me away. In my last moments, please allow me take a vow of sanyas so that I can fulfil my heart's desire before I lose my life.'

His mother gave him the required permission.

Shankara prayed to God who accepted his offering and the crocodile let go his leg; thus the life of Shankara was saved.

Then he spoke to his mother: 'Ma, you gave me permission to take sanyas, so God saved my life. As I have become a sanyasi, I am now leaving home.'

The mother was left with no choice. God's will worked through a crocodile and this is how Shankara fulfilled the mission of his life.

OOO

38. Shivaji

In Indian history the name of Shivaji, the famous Maratha ruler, is remembered with great veneration. His mother, Jija Bai, played a major role in making Shivaji an eminent, distinguished and able warrior. His father was a noble in the kingdom of Bijapur.

Saviour Of Cow

Once, Shivaji was travelling to meet his father. On the way, he saw a meat seller who was about to kill a cow. As taught by his mother, Shivaji had resolved to protect the cow and the holy men.

He said to the man: 'I will pay you the price of this cow, so you better leave her.' But the man refused. At this, Shivaji drew his sword and saved the cow, true to his resolve.

Respect For Women

Shivaji had immense respect for women. Once, he won a battle with a Muslim ruler and his soldiers captured a beautiful Muslim woman and brought her to Shivaji as a gift of victory. Shivaji treated her with great respect and returned her to her people, without any harm or disrespect.

OOO

39. Socrates

Equipoise Of Socrates

Socrates often used to come home late as he was always engrossed in discussing spiritual matters with his friends, admirers and disciples. His wife was unhappy with his late coming.

One day, he was very late at night. His wife, who was extremely annoyed, threw a bucket of cold water on him.

Socrates remained calm and unperturbed and simply said: 'It is like a cloud burst.'

This is an example of equipoise.

Test For Disciples

A disciple once asked Socrates: 'Sir, you ask everyone who wants to become your disciple to look into the pond and tell you what he sees. Why is it so?

Socrates replied: "It is quite simple. One who sees the fish swimming around, I accept him. Others who see their own reflection are in love with their ego. I have no use for them.'

Honesty

Socrates set a wonderful example of honesty and reliability even in the last moments of his life. A few moments before he was to die by drinking a cup of deadly poison, he asked his close friend to repay a small debt he owed to somebody.

Socrates had taken a small loan and even at the time of his death, he remembered his moral obligation to pay back. Besides honesty, this is also an example of calmness and composure of a great man.

Learning Till Death

After having been sentenced to death, Socrates was languishing in prison. One day he heard a fellow prisoner singing a beautiful lyric. Socrates went to him and asked him to teach that lyric.

The prisoner was surprised and asked Socrates why he who had been sentenced to death, wanted to learn that song!

Socrates replied: 'I will be happy if I could learn one thing more before I die!'

Socrates' Triple Test

One day, an acquaintance of Socrates came to him and said: 'Socrates, I want to tell you what I heard about one of your disciples.'

Socrates said: 'Before you tell me, I want to conduct the triple test.'

Socrates continued to say: 'The first test is truth. Have you made sure that what you are going to say is true?'

The man said: 'No, I just heard about it.'

Socrates said: 'So you do not know if it is true or not. Now let us try the second test, which is of goodness. Are you going to tell me something good?'

The man said: 'No.'

Socrates then commented: 'So you want to tell me something bad, without being sure about it.'

The man felt embarrassed.

Socrates said: 'Still there is the third test of usefulness. Is what you want to say going to be useful to me?'

The man said: 'Not, really.'

Then Socrates questioned: 'If what you are going to tell me is neither true, nor good, nor useful, then why tell me at all?'

So if you want to tell something to someone try this Triple Test of Socrates.

OOO

40. S.C. Bose

Helping The Sick

When Subhash was just 19, he took part in a campaign to help victims of Cholera which spread as an epidemic in Cuttack. He and his associates would visit houses of victims to render help. Seeing this some people praised their work but some ruffians made fun of them and also put hurdles in their work. One notorious man Haider was in the forefront to condemn them.

It so happened that some members of the family of Haider also fell victim to the disease. He looked around for medical help but could not get any. On returning home, he found that Subhash and his associates were already helping his family. On seeing this, he felt ashamed and repented for condemning them earlier. He fell at the feet of Subhash and thanked him and his associates for the help rendered.

At this Subhash said: 'Only a human being can help another human being. It is our duty to help someone in their hour of distress and need.'

Haider felt happy and blessed them.

Give Me Blood. I Will Give You Freedom

S.C. Bose occupies a unique position in the history of Indian's struggle for independence. In order to free India from British Raj, he made a scheme to prepare an army of freedom fighters, called Azad Hind Fauj. For this, he needed brave young Indians prepared to sacrifice their lives. So he put an advertisement in some newspapers in response to which a group of young men reached Rangoon (Yangon) where Bose was staying at that time.

A meeting was arranged in a hall where thousands of Indians gathered. Bose made an impressive speech and said: 'You give me your blood, I will give you freedom.'

Several young men and women came forward to sign a letter of confirmation to fight for the country. But Subhash told them to put their signature in blood. Several young men did so and later sacrificed their lives in the fight for freedom from the British rule.

OOO

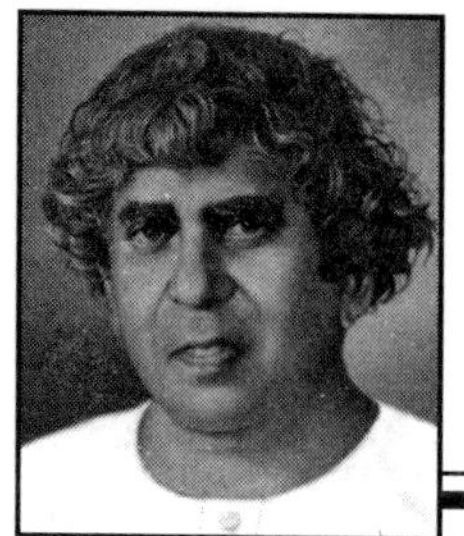

41. Sadhu Vaswani

The Noblest Temple

Sadhu Vaswani served the poor till the last day of his life.

One day, an admirer came to him and gave him a bag full of notes and said: "Dadaji, this is for your temple."

Sadhu Vaswani accepted the money and used it to feed the poor and said: 'The heart of the poor is the noblest temple of God. They get food and bless the name of God.'

Rules Of Service

When one of his disciples asked him about the way of service, Sadhu Vaswani gave him 5 rules of service, as follows:-

1) Perform service silently, without any show and ostentation.

2) Serve humbly and feel grateful to those who gave you a chance to serve them.

3) Serve lovingly. Give with gentleness and without any harshness. Sometimes, when we give a coin to a beggar we also rebuke him.

4) Reform yourself first, and do not interfere with others.

5) Serve without egotism and selfishness. Think yourself as a Tool of God. Do not care for praise and blame.

Honour Women

Sadhu Vaswani, the founder of Mira Movement in Education was a God-loving man who changed the life of many.

When people asked him: 'How did you do it?'

His reply was: 'It was due to my mother.' Then he narrated an incident in his life.

He was leaving home and his mother walked with him until she could walk no further. Then she blessed her son and sought a promise from his son.

'What is it?' asked Vaswani.

'It is nothing very difficult, but you have to promise first,' said the mother. So he promised to do whatever she wanted.

The mother said: 'My child, you are going into a wicked world. Begin everyday with God and close everyday with God.' Then she kissed him and he left.

Sadhu Vaswani said it was his mother's kiss that changed his life and he honoured his promise made to his mother.

Mother is the builder of the home. We should honour women.

❍❍❍

42. Sant Tuka Ram

Control Over Anger

Sant Tuka Ram was a deeply religious person, devoted to God. One day he was carrying a bundle of sugar cane on his head and going towards his home. On the way several children met him and each asked for a sugar cane. He distributed all except one which he brought home. When his wife saw only one sugar cane in his hand, she became furious and started beating Sant Tuka Ram with the same. While she was doing so the sugar cane broke into two pieces.

Sant Tuka Ram laughed at this and said: 'Look you have done a good thing by making two pieces of the sugar cane. You have done my job. Now you take one half and I will take the other half.'

We should keep our anger under control in difficult situations and try to make the best of even the worst times.

OOO

43. Swami Dayananda

Instant Help

Once Swami Dayananda saw a bullock cart caught in a mud track. The driver was beating the bullock hard but the cart wouldn't move as the wheel was stuck deep in the mud. Seeing the plight of the helpless animal, Swamiji jumped into the mud, put his shoulder to the wheel and got the cart moving. The driver was very grateful and went away happy.

Compassion

Swami Dayananda saw a poor woman weeping over the dead body of her son. She had no shroud for the body.

Swamiji gave his own clothing to the woman, to be used as a shroud. This is another example of compassion of a great holy man.

Forgiveness

The founder of Arya Samaj, Swami Dayananda was a great religious and social reformer. He was also a fearless, outspoken, honest and kind man. Some of his opponents conspired to kill him by bribing his cook who mixed deadly poison in Swamiji's food. Consequently, his health deteriorated. When he came to know about the truth, he called his cook, who wept bitterly, apologised and fell at Swamiji's feet.

Swamiji said: 'Listen, if my well-wishers came to know about it, they will surely kill you. So you run away before it is too late.'

ooo

44. Swami Haridas

The great singer Tansen was one of the famous Navratnas of Emperor Akbar. He was a disciple of Swami Haridas who was a great spiritual master and singer.

One morning, Akbar, woke up and decided to walk alone away from his palace. When he reached close to the banks of river Yamuna, he heard an irresistible melodious voice. Swami Haridas, who lived on the banks of the river, was singing devotional songs (Bhajans) in praise of God.

Akbar enjoyed the music in total silence and when the singer finished Akbar went in that direction. He saw Swami Haridas and was mesmerised by his peaceful glowing face radiating happiness. Swami Haridas, immersed in his thoughts, took no note of Akbar's presence.

When he came back to his palace, he asked Tansen: 'You sing well, but why can't you sing like the singer on the river bank?'

Tansen said: 'My lord, I sing for you, the king, but Swami Haridas sings for the king of kings. I am glad that you have heard him, but it is not possible to bring persons like him within the confines of the palace and make him sing in praise of kings. He sings only for God.'

OOO

45. Swami Ram Tirtha

The Whole World Is A School

While going to school, Swami Ram Tirtha used to keep reading a book on the way.

One day, a farmer noticed this and said: 'Son, a book is to be read in the school and not on the track or a field, where you walk and read.'

At this, Ram Tirtha replied: 'For me, the whole world is a school, Sir.'

His reply made the farmer speechless. This is indeed true, that the whole world is a school, where we keep learning all through life.

OOO

46. Swami Vivekananda

Effect Of Words

Once, Swami Vivekananda was giving a discourse to an audience. A critic got up and said: 'All these are mere words which have no effect.' Vivekananda responded by calling that person a fool and also uttered some harsh words. That person got very much annoyed and rushed forward to hit Swamiji.

Vivekananda stopped him, smiled and said: 'Look, this is the effect of words. So words can have effect if listened to carefully and understood well.'

That man understood well, felt ashamed and apologised.

This shows how words can have corresponding effect.

Acquisition Of Knowledge

While in the U.S.A., Swami Vivekananda delivered a series of lectures on spiritual knowledge. A rich doctor was greatly impressed. He requested Vivekananda to transfer some of his knowledge to him instantly for which he was ready to give any amount of money. Vivekananda said he did not need money but the doctor should give instant medical knowledge, in return!

The doctor replied: 'It will take years to impart medical knowledge.'

Vivekananda said: 'In the same way it will take several years to acquire spiritual knowledge.'

It takes years of study and plenty of hard work to acquire knowledge.

Key To Success

Someone asked Vivekananda: 'Swamiji, what is the key to success?'

He replied: 'Take up an idea. Eat that idea, dream that idea and sleep that idea. Be that idea and you will be a success.'

There is only one key to a lock. The key to success lies in doing one task at a time with single-minded devotion.

Faith In God

Swami Vivekananda was invited to visit the U.S.A. to attend the Congress of Religions of the World. While he was sailing on a ship, a foreigner struck acquaintance with Swamiji and came to know about him and the purpose of his visit.

He enquired from Swamiji: 'Where will you stay in America?'

Swamiji said: 'I do not know about it.' And then, in all simplicity added: 'Maybe, I shall stay with you!'

The foreigner was a wealthy person and was going to the same city where the conference was being held. He said without any hesitation: 'Oh, in that case I invite you to stay with us at my place and I shall try to make your stay as comfortable as I can.'

Swamiji had full trust in God. The moral of the story is 'Do your best and trust in God.'

The Way To Peace

A sadhu came to Swami Vivekananda and said: 'Swamiji, I have relinquished everything to attain peace but I have not got it. My mind is always in a turmoil. I went to a guru who gave me a mantra, but that too did not help me. I am perplexed; please guide me.'

Vivekananda looked at him and asked: 'Do you really want peace?'

He said: 'Of course, that is why I have come to you.'

Swamiji said: 'OK. I will tell you the way to peace. Will you do what I say?'

He said: 'Yes, please tell me.'

Swamiji said: 'Leave your home. If you find anyone hungry, feed him. If you meet anyone thirsty, give him water. If you find a sick needy person, get him medicine. Give clothing to the poor. In this way, help the needy, in whatever way you can. By acting in this way, you will get peace.'

The sadhu got the right direction.

By doing service to the needy poor, one can get peace.

OOO

47.
Yudhishtra

True Learning

The guru of the Pandava princes taught a lesson to his disciples: 'Do not get angry.'

Next day, the guru enquired from his students: 'Have you learnt the lesson?'

All the students except Yudhishtra said "Yes."

The guru rebuked him for not learning the lesson and also slapped him.

Yudhishtra remained calm and unperturbed and said: 'Guruji, Yes, I have learned the lesson now!'

Yudhishtra controlled his anger and thus truly learned the lesson, while other princes learned only in theory.

Mind The Swiftest

Lord Yama asked Dharmaraja Yudhishtra: 'What is the swiftest of all in the universe?'

He answered that the mind is the swiftest. The mind can travel at unimaginable speed. That is why it is restless and unpredictable.

It is said that the conquest of mind is the greatest victory.

The Most Surprising

This is an anecdote from the Mahabharata. Yamaraja asked Yudhishtra: 'What is the most surprising thing in this world?'

Yudhishtra replied: 'The most surprising thing is that a person sees his friends, relatives and other persons dying, but he still behaves as if death shall never touch him!'

Death is an inevitable phenomenon, yet most people carry on with their lives, unmindful of its reality. We must realise the significance of life and death, and live life in the knowledge of wisdom of that reality.

The World's Greatest Seers & Philosophers

Amidst modern stress, strife and terrorism, it is imperative to realise what God is really all about. Nothing achieves this objective better than reading about the lives and teachings of the world's greatest seers and philosophers.

Although dealing with metaphysics, the focus of this book is spiritual rather than religious. For spirituality speaks only the language of love, compassion, oneness and bliss. Whatever you may wish to call the Ultimate Reality–God, Brahman, Cosmic Consciousness, Atman–the first-hand experiences and writings of the great seers and philosophers brings home the Truth that every seeker longs for.

Demy size • Pages: 142 • Price: Rs. 120/- • Postage: Rs. 15/-

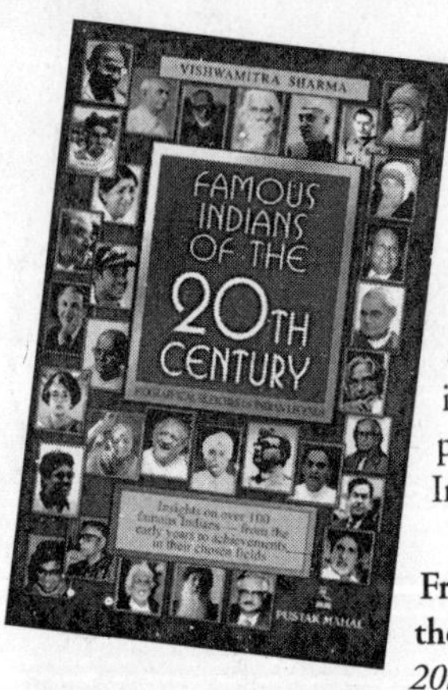

Famous Indians of the 20th Century

For people of all age groups, reading about the lives and times of great Indians is always inspiring and uplifting. This book presents insights on more than 100 famous Indians of the 20th century.

From their early years to achievements in the chosen fields, *Famous Indians of the 20th Century* covers all the relevant details. The book makes excellent reading for students, teachers, parents and all other professionals seeking credible information on the lives and achievements of famous Indians of the 20th century.

Demy size • Pages: 224 • Price: Rs. 120/- • Postage: Rs. 15/-